A C Bevan

De'ATH & DAUGHTERS

Rack Press

First published in 2015 in a limited edition of one hundred and fifty copies, the first fifty numbered and signed by the author.

Acknowledgements are due to the editors of the following publications, in which a number of these poems first appeared: *14; Poetry Salzburg Review; The Delinquent* & *The SHOp*.

The collection was also longlisted in The Poetry School/ Pighog Press Pamphlet Competition 2013.

Published in Wales by Rack Press,
The Rack, Kinnerton, Presteigne, Powys, LD8 2PF
Tel: 01547 560 411
All orders and correspondence: rackpress@nicholasmurray.co.uk

ISBN 978-0-9931045-0-3

Printed by Artisan Print, Presteigne, Powys

EVE

...peeled the apple before she ate it,
cored & pared & separated
into bite-size halves & quarters, pipped
& pitted, & destalked it.

Then she named it: *Golden Russet,*
Maiden's Blush, Sweet Delicious,
Adams Pearmain, Yellow Tremlett's.

Made her pies & crumbles, pressed it
into pomace, sauce, fermented
juices, sparkling wines of moonshine,
applejack & scrumpy cider.

& after several pints of snakebite,
danced stark naked & debauchèd
with a serpent through the orchard.

LEDA

…was out on the boating lake
in pedalo 21,
with her iPod on,
a Cadbury's *Flake*,
& a copy of
Cosmopolitan,

when over the pond
through the sink & sump
of household junk
& used Fetherlite
condoms, swam
   a swan.

Like an upturned gamp
or bumbershoot
gone inside out,
the crook of its neck
   a question mark,
or half a love heart
in search of a mate,

but Leda'd read well,
knew her Greek & Yeats'
'feathered glory…
   …loosening thighs',
drew her can of pepper spray
& Maced it right
between the eyes.

& at the hireman's cry:
'COME IN NUMBER 21
YOUR TIME IS UP!'
the swan held the note
of the last love song
   in its throat,

& went tits up

GODIVA

Twas ye sesounal relegatione battil pon ye Spyon Kop terraces,
of myssyd sytters, loste sixe poynters & nynety mynute swilences,
we were doun amonge ye deade men in tyme addyd on for stoppages.

Botme at Cristemasse, we'd stille a statystycal chaunce of ye graunt ascape
if we bete Unytyd at Heighfeld Rode & othyr resultes wente our wey,
but we nedyd a pooles panell myracle gaing into ye fynal game

with oonli tuo subs & a threedbaar sqwad doun to ye metatarsales
of an undyr-11 academie systeme, a frynge lonee from ye Arsenal,
& clubbe talysman with herte of a lyon but al ye fyrst twich of a camelle.

So it stode at nyl-al & nought to pley for, addyng insulte to injurie tyme
as we teteryd on ye brenke of parachute payements, ye longe declyne &
falle through loure league footeball, ye moodbathe of Mydlands Allyaunce.

Twas then that ye leuedy wif's got ye lytel ehebrows from Byg Ronn,
unpyckyd ye sticch of her replyca kyt & embarkyd pon a masy rynne
ye length of ye parke from dep insyde her owen halfe, skynnyng her man

with notemuge & lolypop, into ye boxe, evadyng eche lungyng takel,
she's droppyd a schuldere then gane doun ouer ye keper's assay to snaffil
ye ball from ye toa of an opene goale, in a kest-iren, naylyd-on, stoonewal

PENALTIE REF!!! shearpe yntayke of breath & he's poyntyd to ye spott,
& ye teleprynter's drummyd its fingres, as she's taken a leggie rynne-up,
plantyd ye wyghte pon her standyng foote & – oh… I can't bere to wacche.

SHEELA-NA-GIG

All the Reverend women priests adore you
as the graven image of motherhood,
as An Bandia Mháthair before you.

Whilst a boy soprano in chasuble
is fondling of father & brotherhood
all the Reverend women priests adore *you*,

splayed above a chapel porch or portal
(albeit pagan in all likelihood
as An Bandia Mháthair before you).

Survivor of Protestant Reformers,
the masons & Magdalene sisterhood,
all the Reverend women priests adore you

& church conservation trusts award you
– like an ancient relic or Norman rood,
as An Bandia Mháthair before you

– protective status, watching over you
from Our Lady of Knock to Holywood,
all the Reverend women priests adore you,
as An Bandia Mháthair before you.

SAINT JOAN

...on this Sunday (*Pray for us*)
Maid of Orléans & Virgin of Donrémy. (*Pray for us*)
Saint Joan conceived in the glory of God (*Pray for us*)
& consecrated in the womb. (*Pray for us*)
Saint Joan as child prodigy (*Pray for us*)
gifted, if somewhat overindulged & away with the fairies, (*Pray for us*)
or on the feast of Corpus Christi (*Pray for us*)
with the underage drinking already. (*Pray for ush!*)
Saint Joan at the difficult age (*Pray for us*)
with your mood swings & menses (*Pray for us*)
alone in your room with *Madonna – those books!* & the voices in your head,
(*Pray for us*)
not to mention the visions & Divine Mission. (*Catherine & Marguerite preserve
us*)
Saint Joan with the brashness of youth, (*Pray for us*)
the anti-authority stance (*Pray for us*)
& frankly bad attitude young lady, or 'Liberator of France'. (*Mon Dieu!*)
I mean, what with the cutting, (*Pray for us*)
brutalist haircut & always in black, & possessed by the Lord knows what
(*Pray for us*)
Saint Joan can you wonder (*Pray for us*)
they thought you sorceress, called you heretic? (*You can't really blame us for
thinking it*)
Saint Joan of all martyrs (*Have mercy on us*)
in your hair shirt of flames & steeple-crowned hat,
Saint Joan at the Auto-da-fé (*Pray for us*)
recanting your recantation. (*Merde Jehanne, fermer la bouche!*)
Saint Joan in the hour of passion (*Pray for us*)
as you prayed to Mary Most Holy at the Place du Vieux Marché
& cried out the name of Our Saviour three times (*Pray for us, Pray for us, Pray
for us!*)
as the curés & cardinals warmed their hands & toasted English muffins,
Saint Joan on that Sunday. (*Pray for us*)
Maid of Orléans & Angel of Donrémy. (*Pray for us*)
Saint Joan of Arc, please pray for us.

MELUSINE

Hook the big one
with a bent pin
& a length of string,

reel her in,
bathing beauty,
tits & fishnet tights,

fantasise: trophy bride,
nuptials with the sea,
jacuzzis,

oysters for breakfast,
lunch & tea,
fish suppers,

surf-

    n-

        turf,

yet up on dry land,
fishwife? slapper?
faded seaside glamour?

think: bycatch, over-
exploited fish stocks,
Kiss-Her-Quick,

throw back

EMILY

Sister, had we known from the off
when we studied the form guide, shouted the odds
& told you put your shirt of purple,
green & white on a racing cert.
My dear, when we said blow the housekeeping,
your silver toffee hammer pin,
amethysts, peridots & pearls,
to hock your hunger strike medal,
& stick the bally lot of it
on the nose of the odds-on favourite
in the big race of the Derby dash –
we'd have put less liquorice in your mash.

Now all the King's horses & all the King's men
                     can't put you together again.

VALEИTIИA

...the *Vostok* valeиtiиe of
Baiкoиия Cosmodяome & gliиt
iи Comяade Khяushchev's
eye, wasи't meяely the fiяst
womaи to ciяcle the eaяth
in oяbital flight – Ouя
Lady of the Satellites; иoя

solely the iиspiяatioи foя
thousaиds of jubilaиt Soviet
womeи fяom Яed Squaяe
to the Baltic States; but

likewise to ███████ & ███████
& ███████ who told me
they иeeded moяe space.

DOLLY

At break of day I will come to thee again!

(Wordsworth: 'Pet Lamb')

The love that dare not bleat its name
shall frolic in the dew again
now I have found the golden fleece,
& clipped from its immortal strain
& shag pile, a single piece

containing all the codes & keys
of DNA, with which to roam
the hillsides, propagate the breed
& map the ovine genome,
with phenotype & chromosome

dyed in the wool of every strand.
I have divided sheep from goat
then spliced again by ewe & ram,
hogget, gimmer, twinter-dam,
through bioengineered design

& begat you my Paschal lamb,
the Chosen One. Bellwether mine,
come mating season, tupping time,
all others will be mutton dressed
for dogging, roasting, shepherds' pie,

compared to thee – as leg & seg,
rack & rump, meat & two veg,
a shambles & an abattoir.
But cosset, breathe a word of this
I'll cut your throat before you baa.

THE VALKYRIUR

Valhalla, Hildr!
& don't spare the horses,
handmaid of stricken
& chooser of slain,
I'm marked for death,
heart in a sling.

Scoop me Sangrida,
I've been in the wars:
fought against mucklewrath,
dragon & battleaxe,
mistletoe arrows with
mortal stings.

Fuck that for a
game of soldiers Mista,
& bear me home on
your vast Wagnerian
bosom, hell-shoon beneath
your wings.

Onward Göndula!
& upward Randgriör!
fly witches, up
to the wild hilltop,
on the back of the blue North
wind.

& over the rainbow
bridge Skeggjöld,
to that crystal palace
of fire & ice,
the Gladhome hearth
of the Norseman Inn.

Bring flagons Skuld,
of the mead of the poets,
& yards of pale
Scandinavian ale,
Skål! Good health!
The fat lady sings.